Dancing Shapes

Ballet and Body Awareness for Young Dancers

D1534542

Dancing Shapes: Ballet and Body Awareness for Young Dancers

by

© 2020 *Once Upon a Dance*

All 2020/2021 book sales will be donated to ballet companies struggling under COVID-19.

All rights reserved. No part of this publication may be reproduced, distributed, or transmitted in any form or by any means, including photocopying, without the prior written permission of the publisher, except in the case of brief quotations embodied in critical reviews and other noncommercial uses permitted by copyright law. Dance teachers are welcome to use images for class instruction; please give *Dancing Shapes* credit.

Summary: Aspiring young dancers learn about Konora's ballet journey and explore the shapes she creates with her body. With more than fifty poses to contemplate or re-create, readers develop an eye for detail as they practice ballet technique; explore movement concepts; and increase body awareness, spatial perception, and balance. Ballet vocabulary, gratitude, and the value of practicing and making healthy choices conclude this first *Dancing Shapes* volume.

ISBN 978-1-7359-8440-7
Main category: Children's Dance
Secondary categories: Ballet Dance, Dancing Reference, Exercise and Fitness for Children, and Children's Books on the Body
First Edition

Back cover photo by Oliver Endahl/Ballet Zaida.

All readers agree to release and hold harmless Once Upon a Dance and all related parties from any claims, causes of action, or liability arising from the contents. Use this book at your own risk.

Other Once Upon a Dance titles: More Dancing Shapes; Nutcracker Dancing Shapes; Konora's Shapes

Thank you

to all who have helped on my ballet journey.

Special shout-outs to:
- *my Emerald Ballet teachers, especially Roman and Erin for the early mornings and late nights, and Sarah, my documentarian*
- *Billy, EBA, and SIDF for the amazing performance opportunities*
- *Roman, Erin, Oliver, Chris, and Steven for the YAGP choreography*
- *Allison and Peter at Ballet West for facilitating my first big opportunity*
- *Nate/Limei for helping me simultaneously graduate and follow my dreams*
- *PNB faculty and staff for a fantastic two (almost) years*
- *my Covid summer teachers who kept me motivated and progressing, especially Pablo*
- *friends who came to the shows and cheered so enthusiastically*
- *the pink tights gang and the ballet squad*
- *my roadies, Andrea and Oona/Tony*
- *my grandparents and family*

Love,

K

Hello Fellow Dancer,

I'm so happy to have you along on this dancing journey. Since I have so much to tell you, I squished at least three books into one!

 The first section is about me and my dancing history. *(page 6)*

 I've included a short warm-up for your muscles and body, feel free to use your own ideas instead. *(page 14)*

 We'll review just a few ballet steps: the five ballet positions, *pliés*, and *relevés*. *(page 15)*

 I've made a pile of dance shapes for you to think about. Hopefully you'll be inspired to re-create them. *(page 21)*

 If you want even more shapes, I've left additional ones on the opposite page and cover. For an extra challenge, figure out which shapes are duplicates from the story's pages and which ones are new.

 If you want to learn more about the French ballet terms, there's a section at the end with translations and how I would pronounce the words. Sometimes I call these ballet words *fancy French*.

So, are you ready to talk dance? Let's go!

Photo: Heidi Leonard

Part One

About Me, Konora

Photo: Oliver Endahl/Ballet Zaida

𝒪𝓃𝒸𝑒 𝒰𝓅𝑜𝓃 𝒶 𝒟𝒶𝓃𝒸𝑒, there was a little girl who dreamed of being a ballerina. She even performed on stage and wore fancy costumes. It felt wonderful to dance for her family and friends, as well as other parents and grandparents. The audience loved to see all the dancers improve and face more challenging roles each year. The audience got to watch the little boys and girls grow up!

Middle photo: Andy Held. Right photo: Wade Heninger/Heninger Fotographik.

Yep, that little girl was me. As I grew, I spent more and more time practicing and performing. I loved dancing on stage with my friends. The pictures above are some of my favorite Nutcracker roles from my years dancing at Emerald Ballet Academy in Washington State.

I've always admired Emerald Ballet's encouragement of all dancers. They invite people of every body type and size. They create on-stage opportunities for all children, including kids with different body parts or ability to dance or learn. They even give boys free classes so more boys will try ballet.

Dance   is   for   everyone!

All photos this page: Wade Heninger/Heninger Fotographik. Thank you to Emerald Ballet Theatre and Roman Zinovyev.

Each year since Emerald Ballet, I've danced in Nutcrackers around the United States, including with the Pacific Northwest Ballet, Aspen Santa Fe Ballet, Ballet West, and Ballet Idaho. I lived in Washington, Colorado, New Mexico, Utah, and Idaho while learning and performing *The Nutcracker.*

Dancing as a paid ballet dancer, even if only for a couple months at a time, was pretty exciting. I felt one step closer to my dream of being a professional ballerina!

Left photo: ©Angela Sterling. Right photo: Mike Reid; choreography by Peter Anastos; costume design by Margaret Mitchell; set design by Christopher McCollum. Bottom photo: Sharen Bradford, The Dancing Image. Thank you Pacific Northwest Ballet, Ballet Idaho, and Aspen Santa Fe Ballet.

Then the coronavirus came, and most of the dancers in the U.S. were sent home. I spent a lot of time dancing in my parents' garage.

My mom and I wanted to make something positive during the crisis, so we created *Once Upon a Dance* and Konora. We made videos of movement stories and songs to help kids stuck at home keep active during such challenging times.

It made me happy to use my imagination and pretend to be Konora. Do you ever pretend to have a different name just for fun? If you had to make up a special dancer name, which name would you choose?

Being Konora reminded me that dance is for everywhere and for everybody. Even though I was sad not to be performing on stage, I realized you can dance almost anytime and almost any place.

You can always use your imagination, and there's a freedom to dancing offstage. Plus, it's incredible to dance in beautiful spaces, like in a field of flowers.

When you are out in the wide world,

it's easier to imagine

you're a fantastical character

with an exciting story.

You could be Mary Poppins

getting ready

to fly off

into the sunset.

Or you could be an ice princess calling out to dolphin friends to bring news of the kingdom.

This is one of my favorite ballet poses, *arabesque*. Are you ready to learn ballet with me?

Warming Up

Before dancing, it's a good idea to warm up your body and muscles. Going through the next part of this book will help do this, but since I want to encourage good dancing habits, let's warm up together.

1) Rub your hands together as if you were making a playdough snake.

2) Give all of your parts a gentle jiggle or shake:
- your hands
- your arms
- your feet
- your legs
- your head
- your shoulders
- your back

3) Bend and straighten your knees ten times.

4) Reach up high, then bend over and try to touch the floor.

5) Draw ten circles in the air using your shoulders as your paintbrushes.

6) Draw circles using each elbow as a paintbrush. Make five little ones and five big ones with each elbow.

7) Draw five little and five gigantic circles with each hand as your paintbrush.

8) Do the same thing with your feet, using your paintbrush toes.

9) Run in place, lifting your knees extra high.

Part Two

Ballet Positions

Ballet technique is a good starting point for all kinds of dance. Students who take a ballet class often begin with the five positions. These basics help us stand tall, find straight legs, and coordinate our body parts in different directions.

Here they are for you to try.

First Position legs and arms

First Position feet

To get into *first position*, stand with your feet together, toes straight ahead. Try to leave your heels, the backs of your feet, together as you open your feet like they're butterfly wings. Imagine a glass of water on your head that you don't want to spill.

For your arms, imagine holding a big ball with your hands in front of your belly button or a little bit higher.

Second position legs and arms

For *second position*, open your arms like you are blowing up a huge balloon, and add space between your heels.

Third position legs and arms
(You could also have one arm high
and one arm side for third position.)

Fourth position legs and arms

Fifth position legs and arms
(You could also have both arms low.)

For *third position*, start in *first* and slide one foot over until your feet look like a spun-around T from above. Bring one arm back in front.

Let's think about *fifth position* next. From *first position* arms and legs, slide your foot to *third* and continue until your heel touches the big toe of your other foot. Arms go above your head, a little in front, where your hair meets your face.

For *fourth position*, slide one foot forward from *fifth*. As you slide your leg to *fourth,* try to imagine you have two headlights on your hips the way a car has lights at the front. Keep your headlights facing forward. Bring one arm lower in front of you.

17

The next thing dancers often learn in ballet is *pliés*. Most of the time, ballet *pliés* are *turned out*, meaning the toes and knees face out, away from each other, while the heels face in. Dancers use *pliés* to create other poses and for turning and jumping.

Here are some pictures of the most important *pliés*. I like to imagine making windows. I pretend birds are coming, and they need lots of room to fly through.

Second position *plié*
Second position arms

First position *plié*

Third position *plié*
Third position arms

There are also *grand pliés*, where we bend our knees more and go lower.

We try to keep the rest of our body in the same shape as we go down.

In *second position*, we keep the bottoms of our feet on the floor.

In the other positions, we lift our heels up as we descend and bend our knees. It helps to imagine that glass of water is still on our head, and we're trying not to spill it.

Second position *grand pliés*
Stretched arms help us think of going wide.

First position *grand pliés*
Fifth position arms help us stay tall.

Please hold on to something when you try these *relevés* with legs in *first* and *second positions*.

With ballet, most of the time our feet and legs are *turned out,* even when we are in *relevé.*

If all our toes point forward with the heels in back, we call it parallel position. Watch for both *turned out* and parallel feet in the next section.

Part Three
Thinking about Details

When we think about ballet poses, we think about the shapes' details. We think about legs, feet, arms, hands, directions, and keeping our backs straight to do the five positions, *pliés,* and *relevés.*

When we try to create any shape, we look at individual body parts. But even if we know how all the parts should look, some shapes are just really tricky, and it takes a lot of practice to get them just right or to be able to do them at all.

Others are simple and can even be relaxing.

When I started thinking about shapes, I realized how many unique ones you can make with your body.

I   think   it   must   be   close   to   infinity!

Let's make more shapes together! Would you imagine you're an animal while you try the next six shapes? Which animal are you?

By the way, there isn't one right answer for these. I showed my family this one, and they suggested snake, cobra, walrus, seal, and sea lion.

This position helps stretch and strengthen your back.

Do the legs on this page remind you of a ballet position we learned?

Even when we aren't exactly doing ballet, it can help us find the position and balance.

Notice we have one leg *turned out* and one that's parallel?

Remember when the ice princess made the *arabesque*?
We're finding that *arabesque* leg here.

Are our feet *turned out* or parallel? Notice our fingers and toes point the same direction.

That's the end of my animals. As we explore more shapes, feel free to see if any remind you of a critter or anything else. It's fun to add a little story when we make or copy shapes.

Let's think more about hands and feet in these pictures.

In the first picture, both my hands and feet are flexed.

In the second picture, my feet are pointed.
We might say our hands are extended or reaching
instead of calling them pointed, but it's a similar idea.

These poses are a little hard to make. Do you want to give it a try?

Always be gentle with your body. Don't do anything that hurts. Having fun and doing what works for you
are important!

Let's keep thinking about the details we can make with our hands.
Here are some ways I can use my fingers, thumbs, and wrists to make different shapes.
I can make

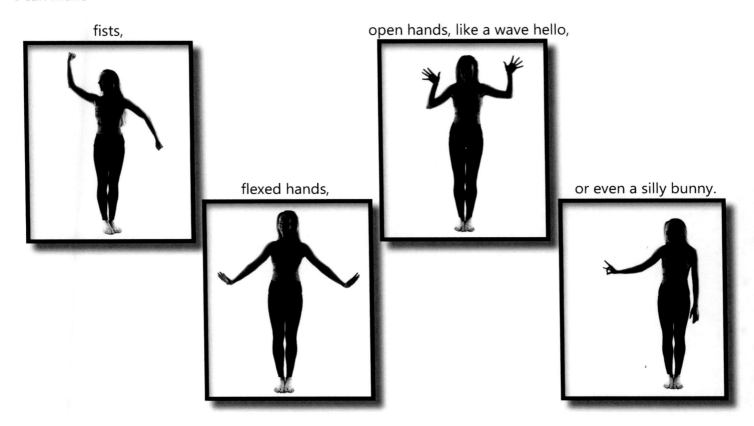

fists,

open hands, like a wave hello,

flexed hands,

or even a silly bunny.

Let's think about arms and legs and how we can bend, straighten or curve them.

In the first picture,
I have one straight leg and
one bent leg with straight arms.

In the second picture,
I have straight legs with curved arms.

In the third picture,
I have bent legs and straight arms.

Did you make these shapes? Do you have a favorite shape that we've made so far?

Do you remember which picture above has second position feet? Which pictures show flexed hands?

Try these two.
Are our knees and arms straight, bent, or curved?

Another thing to think about is how we connect to the floor. Which body parts touch the floor, and how much weight is on those parts? In these pictures, weight means how much do we feel like we're standing on each foot? Is it the same on both feet, or do we have more weight on one foot?

Don't forget our backs and our heads. We can make Curves with our backs too.

Even our eyes and where we look or focus can give a pose a different feeling.

It's fascinating to see how shapes can look so different with just one change.

In one picture, I've tipped or tilted my upper body, the top half of me, while leaving the bottom half of my body the same.

33

On the following pages are more shapes for you to copy.

- What are our arms, hands, and fingers doing?
Which direction are they compared to our bodies and each other?

- What are our legs, feet, and toes doing?
Are our legs *turned out*, parallel, or somewhere in between?
Are our feet pointed, flexed, or something else?

- Think about the angle or tilt of the body.

- Are there any curves or bends?

- What about our heads?

- What's our focus? Where are our eyes looking?

With so many details, it's hard to know where to begin. Looking at feet or hands is one good way to start. Let's think about this shape together.

• My feet are in a wide *second position,* so of course, my legs and feet are *turned out.*

• I've lifted my heel, and there's about as much weight in those toes as in my whole other foot.

• Both arms and one leg are straight. One leg is slightly bent, about the amount of a *plié* bend.

• My hands are in line with my arms; the wrists don't flex or bend.

• My palms, the insides of my hands, face down and out.

• My thumbs are below my fingers.

• My head faces straight ahead.

• My eyes look straight ahead.

Don't forget about focus. If
you can't tell from the picture,
make your best guess.

On this page, one foot has all of the weight. When we stand without doing a *relevé*, we stand on flexed feet.

In ballet, our feet usually point when they leave the floor. The other feet in these two pictures are pointed.

With harder shapes, particularly if you have to balance on one leg, it might be helpful to sit and create the top half of the body first.

Or you could hold on to something for a little balance help.

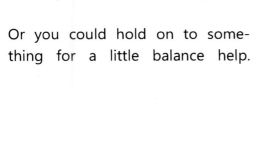

Even if you can't do all of the poses yet, you are working your brain just by thinking about them.

You don't have to look like me or be able to do the shapes I do to call yourself a dancer.

You might find it helpful to take pictures of your shapes and compare them to mine sometime. Dancers often use mirrors that stretch across an entire side of the dance studio to help them fine-tune their shapes during classes and rehearsals. Self-observation and feedback are valuable parts of practice.

Part Four

Saying Thanks

Did you know that much of what I do as a ballerina is practice the same steps over and over and over and over again?

When we learn choreography (sequences of shapes and movements), we do it over and over to get better and stronger.

Nothing gets perfect. We keep moving and improving We're kind of like that little fish in *Finding Nemo*,

"Just keep swimming, just keep swimming."

We just keep moving.

I hope you practice your shapes again some time. I'll be practicing mine almost every day.

I'm glad my body is strong and can make so many magnificent shapes.

I try to take good care of my body since it works so hard for me. Getting good sleep, eating a variety of healthy foods, and making safe choices, like wearing helmets and seatbelts, are all ways I thank my body.

At the end of a class we take a ballet curtsy or bow to thank everyone.

We thank our teacher for teaching us.

We thank the pianist if we are lucky enough to have an in-class musician play for us.

We also thank ourselves and our friends for being there and working hard.

 **Thank you** for being here and being you.

Thank you so much for thinking about these concepts and for working your body and brain with me. I'm delighted you joined me. Dancing is often more fun with a friend.

I love creating dance, going on adventures, and telling stories with my ballet. I'll be making more shapes and writing down some of my favorite dancing stories. I hope we can go on dancing adventures together soon.

Until then, **hugs**, happy dancing, and stay safe.

Love,

 *Konora*

Fancy French

- arabesque ['air-a-BESK'] a decorative pattern of intertwined flowing lines
- plié ['plee-AY'] bend (bent/bending)
- grand plié ['grahn plee-AY'] big bend
- relevé ['rehl-i-VAY'] raise (raised)

Positions and Concepts Review

- first position
- second position
- third position
- fourth position
- fifth position
- turned out and parallel
- pointed and flexed
- bent, straight, and curved
- connection to the floor
- weight
- focus
- tipped (tilted)

Coming Up Next

Watch for *More Dancing Shapes* where we'll explore:

- different ballet positions and poses
- storytelling
- floor shapes and more

Grown-ups can subscribe at *www.OnceUponADance.com*. Watch for subscriber bonus content.

We'd jump for joy and appreciate a positive review from a grown-up at amazon.com or goodreads.com.

We're a mom and daughter duo who were both happily immersed in the ballet world until March 2020. We spent the spring and summer learning InDesign and book publishing, and this project has been a labor of love. It would mean the world to know it made someone happy.

Once Upon a Dance was created during COVID-19.

Konora is a Professional Division student
at Pacific Northwest Ballet.

Konora's mother taught creative movement and ballet for twenty years and was honored to be chosen and recognized by her local City Council for *embodying the spirit of partnership and commitment to children in our community* for her work with young dancers.

Visit **www.OnceUponADance.com** to subscribe
and for information on other titles:
More Dancing Shapes
Nutcracker Dancing Shapes
Dancing Shapes with Attitude
Konora's Shapes
More Konora's Shapes
Ballerina Dreams Journal
Dancing Shapes Journal
Joey Finds His Jump!
Petunia Perks Up

Made in the USA
Las Vegas, NV
30 April 2021

22269435R00033